PRINCEWILL LAGANG

Beyond the Berkshire Hathaway: Warren Buffett's Impact on Finance and Philanthropy

First published by PRINCEWILL LAGANG 2023

Copyright © 2023 by Princewill Lagang

All rights reserved. No part of this publication may be reproduced, stored or transmitted in any form or by any means, electronic, mechanical, photocopying, recording, scanning, or otherwise without written permission from the publisher. It is illegal to copy this book, post it to a website, or distribute it by any other means without permission.

Princewill Lagang asserts the moral right to be identified as the author of this work.

First edition

This book was professionally typeset on Reedsy. Find out more at reedsy.com

Contents

1. Introduction — 1
2. The Beginning — 3
3. Warren Buffett's Investment Philosophy — 7
4. Warren Buffett's Philanthropic Journey — 11
5. Leadership and Legacy: The Buffett Effect — 15
6. The Cultural Impact of Berkshire Hathaway — 18
7. The Evolution of Finance: Navigating the New Normal — 22
8. Warren Buffett's Enduring Legacy — 26
9. Synthesis and Future Perspectives — 30
10. Reflections and Invitations — 33
11. Beyond Buffett - Charting a New Course — 36
12. The Legacy Unfolds - A Continuous Journey — 39
13. Summary — 43

1

Introduction

Welcome to "Buffett's Legacy: Wisdom, Wealth, and a Changing World." In the pages that follow, we embark on an illuminating exploration of the life and enduring influence of one of the most iconic figures in finance—Warren Buffett, the Oracle of Omaha.

This journey unfolds in twelve chapters, each dedicated to unraveling a distinct facet of Buffett's legacy. We begin by peering into the financial mastery that propelled Buffett to the pinnacle of success, dissecting the investment principles that transformed Berkshire Hathaway into a conglomerate for the ages.

But this exploration goes beyond balance sheets and stock markets. We delve into Buffett's philanthropic journey, tracing the profound impact of his commitment to giving back on a global scale. We dissect the unique leadership style that has made Berkshire Hathaway a cultural icon and examine the conglomerate's role in shaping the business world.

As we navigate through the chapters, we reflect on the changing landscape of finance in the 21st century, exploring technological disruptions, evolving leadership paradigms, and the rise of sustainable finance. This isn't just a retrospective; it's an invitation to ponder the implications of Buffett's legacy for the future.

"Buffett's Legacy" is more than a book—it's a journey into the wisdom, wealth, and philanthropy that define the Oracle of Omaha. Whether you're an investor, a leader, or someone seeking inspiration for navigating life's complexities, join us as we unravel the layers of Buffett's impact and contemplate the lessons for a changing world. Welcome to a narrative that goes beyond finance, offering insights that endure across generations.

2

The Beginning

Title: Beyond the Berkshire Hathaway: Warren Buffett's Impact on Finance and Philanthropy

In the world of finance, few names carry as much weight and reverence as Warren Buffett. Often referred to as the "Oracle of Omaha," Buffett is not just a successful investor and business magnate; he is a living legend whose influence extends far beyond the boardrooms and trading floors. This chapter delves into the early life of Warren Buffett, the foundation of his financial principles, and the profound impact he has made on the realms of finance and philanthropy.

1.1 Background and Early Life

1.1.1 Humble Beginnings in Omaha

Warren Edward Buffett was born on August 30, 1930, in Omaha, Nebraska. Raised during the Great Depression, Buffett displayed an early aptitude for numbers and an entrepreneurial spirit. His first foray into business was delivering newspapers, and by the age of 11, he had purchased his first stock—

Cities Service Preferred—at a mere $38 per share.

1.1.2 Formative Years and Investment Prowess

Buffett's interest in investing only deepened during his teenage years. He devoured books on the subject, including works by Benjamin Graham, whose philosophy of value investing would become a cornerstone of Buffett's own approach. After completing his education at the University of Nebraska and later at Columbia Business School, Buffett worked for Graham's investment firm, Graham-Newman Corporation, marking the beginning of his professional journey in finance.

1.2 The Birth of Berkshire Hathaway

1.2.1 Transformative Partnership: Buffett and Munger

In 1965, Buffett acquired a textile manufacturing company named Berkshire Hathaway. While the textile business itself proved challenging, the acquisition marked a turning point in Buffett's career. It also marked the beginning of his long-lasting partnership with Charlie Munger, a relationship that would prove instrumental in shaping Berkshire Hathaway into the conglomerate it is today.

1.2.2 The Berkshire Mystique

Under Buffett's leadership, Berkshire Hathaway evolved from a struggling textile company into a diversified multinational conglomerate. Buffett's approach to investing, characterized by a focus on intrinsic value and a long-term perspective, became the hallmark of Berkshire's success. The annual shareholder letters written by Buffett became revered for their wisdom and insights, creating a unique mystique around the company.

1.3 The Sage of Omaha's Investment Philosophy

1.3.1 Value Investing and Margin of Safety

Buffett's investment philosophy is rooted in the principles of value investing. He seeks out companies with strong fundamentals, durable competitive advantages, and competent management. The concept of a "margin of safety," emphasizing the importance of buying stocks at a significant discount to their intrinsic value, has been a guiding principle in Buffett's investment decisions.

1.3.2 Long-Term Vision and Patience

Buffett's unparalleled success is not only attributed to his financial acumen but also to his long-term perspective. He famously stated, "Our favorite holding period is forever." This patient approach to investing has allowed him to weather market fluctuations and capitalize on the compounding power of time.

1.4 Beyond the Balance Sheet: Buffett's Philanthropic Legacy

1.4.1 The Giving Pledge

In addition to his achievements in finance, Warren Buffett has become a symbol of philanthropy. In 2006, he made headlines with his decision to donate the majority of his wealth to the Bill and Melinda Gates Foundation. Buffett, along with Bill and Melinda Gates, launched the Giving Pledge in 2010—a commitment by some of the world's wealthiest individuals to give away the majority of their wealth to address society's most pressing problems.

1.4.2 Bridging the Wealth Gap

Buffett's philanthropy extends beyond monetary contributions. His advocacy for equitable wealth distribution and calls for higher taxes on the wealthy have sparked conversations about social responsibility in the business world. This chapter explores how Buffett's commitment to philanthropy has influenced not only the causes he supports but also the broader conversation about the role of wealth in society.

1.5 Structure of the Book

As we embark on this exploration of Warren Buffett's impact on finance and philanthropy, subsequent chapters will delve deeper into specific aspects of his life and career. From his approach to stock picking to the intricacies of his philanthropic endeavors, this book aims to provide a comprehensive understanding of the man behind the Berkshire Hathaway empire and the far-reaching implications of his influence.

3

Warren Buffett's Investment Philosophy

3.1 The Foundations of Value Investing

3.1.1 Benjamin Graham's Influence

To understand Warren Buffett's investment philosophy, it is essential to trace its roots to his mentor, Benjamin Graham. This section explores the principles of value investing that Buffett absorbed during his time at Columbia Business School and while working for Graham. The emphasis on intrinsic value, margin of safety, and a disciplined approach to investing laid the groundwork for Buffett's future success.

3.1.2 Departures from the Grahamian Path

While Buffett adheres to many of Graham's principles, he has also evolved and refined his investment philosophy. This section delves into the key departures from Graham's approach, such as the emphasis on the quality of the business and the concept of investing in companies with durable competitive advantages.

3.2 The Moat: Buffett's Key to Sustainable Success

3.2.1 Identifying Economic Moats

At the core of Buffett's investment strategy is the concept of an economic moat—an enduring competitive advantage that protects a company from competitors. This section explores the various types of economic moats, including brand strength, cost advantages, network effects, and regulatory advantages. Case studies of companies with strong moats provide insights into how Buffett assesses and values these competitive advantages.

3.2.2 Case Studies: Coca-Cola and See's Candies

Two iconic investments, Coca-Cola and See's Candies, exemplify Buffett's focus on economic moats. This section analyzes these investments, examining how the companies' brand strength and market positions contributed to their economic moats and long-term success within the Berkshire Hathaway portfolio.

3.3 The Long-Term Horizon: Patient Capital at Work

3.3.1 Compound Interest and Time

Warren Buffett famously said, "The stock market is designed to transfer money from the active to the patient." This section explores Buffett's commitment to a long-term investment horizon and the compounding power of time. Through examples from his own portfolio, including the acquisition of Geico and the holding of American Express, readers gain insights into how patience has been a key driver of Berkshire Hathaway's success.

3.3.2 Weathering Market Fluctuations

Buffett's long-term perspective is tested during market fluctuations. This section examines specific instances, such as the dot-com bubble and the 2008 financial crisis, where Buffett's patience and commitment to intrinsic value allowed Berkshire Hathaway to not only weather the storms but emerge stronger.

3.4 Risk Management and the Berkshire Approach

3.4.1 The Importance of Margin of Safety

Central to Buffett's risk management strategy is the concept of a margin of safety. This section delves into how Buffett defines and applies the margin of safety, exploring its role in protecting investments from unexpected downturns and market volatility.

3.4.2 The Berkshire Hathaway Insurance Advantage

Berkshire Hathaway's ownership of insurance companies, including GEICO and General Re, plays a crucial role in its risk management strategy. This section examines how the insurance float generated by these companies provides Berkshire with a unique advantage, allowing it to deploy capital opportunistically and navigate market uncertainties.

3.5 The Behavioral Economics of Warren Buffett

3.5.1 Emotions and Cognitive Biases

Warren Buffett's success is not solely attributed to financial acumen but also to an understanding of human behavior. This section explores how Buffett navigates the emotional and psychological aspects of investing, recognizing and mitigating cognitive biases that can lead to suboptimal decision-making.

3.5.2 Mr. Market and Contrarian Thinking

Buffett often references Mr. Market, a fictional character representing the irrationality of the stock market. This section examines how Buffett's contrarian thinking allows him to capitalize on market inefficiencies, making investment decisions based on fundamentals rather than short-term market sentiment.

3.6 The Evolution of Buffett's Portfolio

3.6.1 Shifts in Sector Emphasis

Over the years, Buffett's portfolio has evolved, reflecting changes in the economic landscape and his investment philosophy. This section explores notable shifts in sector emphasis, from an initial focus on classic value stocks to more recent investments in technology companies like Apple.

3.6.2 The Berkshire Hathaway Stock: A Testament to Faith

Warren Buffett's preference for holding onto stocks for the long term extends to his own company's stock. This section examines the dynamics of Berkshire Hathaway's stock, exploring why Buffett discourages stock splits and the significance of the company's Class A and Class B shares.

3.7 Lessons for Investors

3.7.1 Applying Buffett's Wisdom

The chapter concludes with a reflection on the key lessons investors can draw from Warren Buffett's investment philosophy. Whether emphasizing the importance of a long-term perspective, understanding economic moats, or managing risk, Buffett's approach provides a roadmap for investors seeking sustainable success in the dynamic world of finance.

4

Warren Buffett's Philanthropic Journey

4.1 The Origins of Buffett's Philanthropy

4.1.1 A Pledge to Give Back

Warren Buffett's commitment to philanthropy is as legendary as his prowess in finance. This section delves into the early influences and experiences that shaped Buffett's philanthropic values. From his childhood lessons in generosity to witnessing the impact of his father's charitable acts, readers gain insight into the roots of Buffett's dedication to giving back.

4.1.2 The Turning Point: The Gates Foundation

A pivotal moment in Buffett's philanthropic journey occurred in 2006 when he announced his decision to donate the majority of his wealth to the Bill and Melinda Gates Foundation. This section explores the events and conversations that led to this transformative pledge, highlighting the alignment of values between Buffett and the Gateses in addressing global issues.

4.2 The Giving Pledge: A Call to Action

4.2.1 Rallying the Wealthy

In 2010, Warren Buffett, along with Bill and Melinda Gates, initiated the Giving Pledge—a commitment by some of the world's wealthiest individuals to dedicate the majority of their wealth to address society's most pressing problems. This section examines the inception of the Giving Pledge, its mission, and the influential figures who have joined the cause, emphasizing the collective responsibility of the wealthy to contribute to the greater good.

4.2.2 Stories of Impact: Giving Pledge Signatories

The chapter highlights stories of select Giving Pledge signatories, showcasing their diverse philanthropic initiatives. From healthcare and education to environmental conservation, the section provides a glimpse into how these individuals are leveraging their wealth to make a positive impact on a global scale.

4.3 The Buffett-Gates Partnership

4.3.1 A Shared Vision for Global Impact

Warren Buffett's collaboration with the Gates Foundation extends beyond financial contributions. This section explores the shared vision of Buffett and the Gateses in tackling global challenges such as poverty, disease, and lack of access to education. It delves into specific initiatives and projects supported by Buffett's contributions, emphasizing the strategic alignment of their philanthropic efforts.

4.3.2 Leveraging Business Acumen for Social Change

Buffett's background in business and investing has influenced the way he approaches philanthropy. This section examines how Buffett applies his business acumen to maximize the effectiveness of his charitable giving, from strategic grant-making to encouraging innovative solutions to social issues.

4.4 Bridging the Wealth Gap: Buffett's Advocacy

4.4.1 Calls for Responsible Wealth Distribution

Warren Buffett is not just a philanthropist; he is a vocal advocate for responsible wealth distribution. This section explores Buffett's public statements and letters addressing the need for the wealthy to contribute more to society. It analyzes his calls for fair taxation and the importance of narrowing the wealth gap for the benefit of society as a whole.

4.4.2 The Buffett Rule and Tax Reform

Buffett's advocacy for tax reform, particularly the "Buffett Rule," which proposes higher taxes on the wealthiest individuals, has sparked national conversations. This section delves into the rationale behind the Buffett Rule, its reception in the political landscape, and the ongoing dialogue about the role of the wealthy in funding essential public services.

4.5 Lessons in Effective Philanthropy

4.5.1 Strategic Giving: Beyond Writing Checks

Warren Buffett's philanthropic journey offers valuable lessons for individuals and organizations engaged in giving. This section explores the concept of strategic philanthropy, emphasizing the importance of thoughtful giving, measurable impact, and collaboration with other philanthropists and organizations.

4.5.2 The Ripple Effect: Inspiring a New Generation

The chapter concludes by examining the ripple effect of Warren Buffett's philanthropy on future generations of investors and philanthropists. From the Giving Pledge to the influence on socially conscious investing, Buffett's impact extends beyond his financial contributions, shaping the landscape of philanthropy for years to come.

As we continue to unravel the multifaceted legacy of Warren Buffett, subsequent chapters will explore additional dimensions of his life, examining his leadership style, the cultural impact of Berkshire Hathaway, and the ongoing evolution of his philosophy in a rapidly changing world.

5

Leadership and Legacy: The Buffett Effect

5.1 The Leadership Style of Warren Buffett

5.1.1 Decentralized Decision-Making

Warren Buffett's leadership style is characterized by a commitment to decentralized decision-making. This section explores how Buffett empowers the managers of Berkshire Hathaway's subsidiaries, fostering a culture of trust and autonomy. Through case studies of specific companies within the Berkshire portfolio, readers gain insights into the benefits and challenges of this leadership approach.

5.1.2 The Importance of Integrity

Integrity is a cornerstone of Buffett's leadership philosophy. This section examines how Buffett's commitment to honesty and transparency has contributed to the trust placed in him by shareholders, employees, and the broader business community. Case studies highlight instances where integrity played a pivotal role in decision-making within Berkshire Hathaway.

5.2 The Buffett Effect on Corporate Culture

5.2.1 Values-Driven Culture

Berkshire Hathaway is renowned for its unique corporate culture, shaped by the values instilled by Warren Buffett. This section explores the principles that define the Berkshire culture, including a focus on long-term thinking, accountability, and a sense of stewardship. Case studies showcase how these values manifest in day-to-day operations and decision-making across the conglomerate.

5.2.2 The Shareholder Connection

Buffett's commitment to shareholder value is a central tenet of Berkshire Hathaway's culture. This section examines the ways in which Buffett prioritizes shareholder interests, from his emphasis on transparency in communication to his advocacy for fair treatment of shareholders. Case studies illustrate how this shareholder-centric approach has contributed to the longevity and success of Berkshire Hathaway.

5.3 Challenges and Criticisms

5.3.1 Succession Planning Concerns

While Buffett's leadership has been instrumental in Berkshire's success, succession planning remains a critical challenge. This section explores the concerns and criticisms surrounding the issue of leadership transition within the conglomerate. It examines Berkshire's approach to addressing succession planning and the potential impact on the company's future.

5.3.2 Critiques of the Buffett Model

Buffett's investment and leadership model is not without its critics. This section delves into the criticisms leveled against Buffett's strategies, from accusations of conservatism to debates about the conglomerate's capital allocation decisions. An objective analysis of these critiques provides a comprehensive view of the strengths and weaknesses of the Buffett model.

5.4 The Evolution of Buffett's Leadership

5.4.1 Adapting to Change

As the business landscape evolves, so too does Buffett's approach to leadership. This section explores how Buffett has adapted his leadership style in response to technological advancements, changes in consumer behavior, and other external factors. Case studies highlight specific instances where Berkshire Hathaway has embraced innovation while maintaining its core principles.

5.4.2 Lessons for Aspiring Leaders

The chapter concludes by distilling key leadership lessons from Warren Buffett's journey. Whether emphasizing the importance of integrity, the value of long-term thinking, or the role of adaptability, Buffett's leadership provides valuable insights for aspiring leaders in any industry.

As we delve further into the legacy of Warren Buffett, subsequent chapters will explore the cultural impact of Berkshire Hathaway on the business world, the philanthropic endeavors of Buffett and his contemporaries, and the ongoing relevance of his investment philosophy in a rapidly changing financial landscape.

6

The Cultural Impact of Berkshire Hathaway

6.1 Berkshire Hathaway as a Cultural Icon

6.1.1 The Berkshire Mystique

Berkshire Hathaway has transcended its status as a conglomerate to become a cultural icon. This section explores the unique allure of Berkshire Hathaway, examining how the annual shareholder meetings, Warren Buffett's shareholder letters, and the company's reputation for long-term value creation have contributed to its mystique. The impact of the Berkshire brand on popular culture and the investment community is analyzed.

6.1.2 The Shareholder Community

The annual pilgrimage of shareholders to Omaha for the Berkshire Hathaway Annual Meeting has become a hallmark of the company's culture. This section delves into the sense of community among Berkshire shareholders, the camaraderie that exists at the annual meeting, and the ways in which this unique shareholder culture has contributed to the company's identity.

6.2 The Berkshire Hathaway Model and Business Ethics

6.2.1 Corporate Governance and Transparency

Berkshire Hathaway is often cited as a model for good corporate governance. This section examines the company's governance structure, emphasizing the role of transparency, accountability, and ethical business practices in shaping Berkshire's corporate identity. Case studies highlight instances where Berkshire's commitment to these principles has been tested and upheld.

6.2.2 Business Ethics in Action

From the careful selection of ethical business partners to the emphasis on long-term relationships, this section explores how Berkshire Hathaway's business ethics have played a crucial role in its success. Case studies examine specific instances where ethical considerations influenced business decisions and the broader impact of these decisions on Berkshire's reputation.

6.3 The Berkshire Hathaway Effect on Investment Strategies

6.3.1 The Buffett Model's Influence

Warren Buffett's investment philosophy has had a profound impact on the broader investment community. This section examines how the "Buffett model" has influenced individual investors, fund managers, and the financial industry at large. It explores the adoption of value investing principles, long-term thinking, and risk management strategies inspired by Buffett's approach.

6.3.2 The Rise of Berkshire-Like Conglomerates

Berkshire Hathaway's success has inspired the formation of other conglomerates seeking to replicate its model. This section explores the emergence of Berkshire-like conglomerates, analyzing their strategies, successes, and challenges. It examines the factors that contribute to the appeal of the conglomerate model and the ways in which these entities navigate the complexities of diverse business holdings.

6.4 Challenges to the Berkshire Legacy

6.4.1 Navigating Technological Disruption

In an era of rapid technological change, Berkshire Hathaway faces challenges to its traditional business model. This section explores how the conglomerate is navigating the impact of technological disruption on its diverse portfolio, from traditional industries like insurance and manufacturing to emerging sectors such as technology and renewable energy.

6.4.2 Maintaining Cultural Integrity

As Berkshire Hathaway evolves, there are concerns about maintaining the cultural integrity that has defined the company. This section examines the challenges of balancing tradition with innovation, the potential tensions between decentralization and centralized decision-making, and the steps Berkshire is taking to ensure the continuity of its cultural impact.

6.5 Lessons from Berkshire's Cultural Impact

6.5.1 Enduring Principles

The chapter concludes by distilling key lessons from the cultural impact of Berkshire Hathaway. Whether emphasizing the importance of transparency, ethical business practices, or the enduring appeal of the Berkshire mystique, the cultural legacy of Berkshire Hathaway provides valuable insights for businesses and investors seeking long-term success in a dynamic and ever-changing environment.

As we continue to explore the multifaceted legacy of Warren Buffett, subsequent chapters will delve into the philanthropic endeavors of Buffett and his contemporaries, the evolving landscape of finance, and the ongoing relevance of Buffett's investment philosophy in a rapidly changing world.

7

The Evolution of Finance: Navigating the New Normal

7.1 The Changing Landscape of Finance

7.1.1 Technological Disruption

The financial industry is undergoing rapid transformation driven by technological advancements. This section explores how innovations such as fintech, blockchain, and artificial intelligence are reshaping traditional financial models. The impact of these changes on investment strategies, risk management, and market dynamics is analyzed, with a focus on how Berkshire Hathaway and Warren Buffett have adapted to this new financial landscape.

7.1.2 Globalization and Economic Interconnectedness

The increasing interconnectedness of global economies presents both opportunities and challenges for investors. This section examines how globalization has influenced investment decisions, portfolio diversification, and risk assessment. Case studies explore specific instances where Berkshire Hathaway has navigated the complexities of a globally interconnected financial system.

7.2 Berkshire Hathaway in the Digital Age

7.2.1 Embracing Technological Innovation

As technology becomes a driving force in the economy, Berkshire Hathaway is faced with the challenge of embracing innovation while staying true to its core principles. This section explores how Berkshire Hathaway has incorporated technology into its investment portfolio, the acquisition of technology-focused companies, and the ways in which Warren Buffett views the role of technology in Berkshire's future.

7.2.2 Impact on Investment Decision-Making

The chapter delves into how technological advancements have influenced Berkshire's investment decision-making process. From the use of data analytics to the incorporation of machine learning algorithms, this section examines the ways in which technology has enhanced the analytical capabilities of Berkshire Hathaway and the potential risks associated with increased reliance on data-driven strategies.

7.3 Sustainable Finance and Social Responsibility

7.3.1 The Rise of Sustainable Investing

There is a growing emphasis on sustainable and socially responsible investing. This section explores the shift toward sustainable finance, examining how environmental, social, and governance (ESG) factors are increasingly considered in investment decisions. Case studies highlight instances where Berkshire Hathaway has addressed ESG considerations and the broader implications for the future of finance.

7.3.2 Philanthropy as a Driver of Change

Warren Buffett's commitment to philanthropy has not only influenced the financial industry but has also contributed to a broader conversation about the role of wealth in society. This section explores how philanthropy is becoming a driving force for change in finance, influencing investment priorities, corporate governance, and the expectations placed on wealthy individuals and corporations.

7.4 The Future of Finance: Challenges and Opportunities

7.4.1 Regulatory Challenges

As the financial industry evolves, it faces increasing scrutiny and regulatory challenges. This section examines the regulatory landscape, exploring how changes in financial regulations impact Berkshire Hathaway's operations and investment strategies. It also analyzes the potential implications of regulatory developments on the broader financial ecosystem.

7.4.2 Opportunities in Disruption

While challenges abound, there are also opportunities for innovation and growth in the evolving financial landscape. This section explores how Berkshire Hathaway is positioning itself to capitalize on emerging opportunities, from investments in disruptive technologies to strategic partnerships that leverage the strengths of traditional and new financial models.

7.5 The Continuing Legacy of Warren Buffett

7.5.1 Adapting to Change

Warren Buffett's legacy is not only defined by past successes but also by the ability to adapt to change. This section reflects on how Buffett's principles and investment philosophy continue to guide Berkshire Hathaway through the complexities of the modern financial world. It examines the ongoing relevance of Buffett's wisdom in navigating the challenges and opportunities that lie ahead.

7.5.2 Inspiring the Next Generation

The chapter concludes by exploring how Warren Buffett's legacy is inspiring the next generation of investors, entrepreneurs, and philanthropists. Whether through the principles outlined in his shareholder letters, the philanthropic initiatives he championed, or the cultural impact of Berkshire Hathaway, Buffett's influence extends beyond his own lifetime, shaping the future of finance and philanthropy.

As we approach the conclusion of this exploration, subsequent chapters will offer a comprehensive reflection on the multifaceted legacy of Warren Buffett, examining his impact on individuals, industries, and society at large.

8

Warren Buffett's Enduring Legacy

8.1 The Personal Impact of Warren Buffett

8.1.1 Mentorship and Education

Warren Buffett's influence extends beyond the realm of finance. This section explores the personal impact of Buffett on individuals who have looked to him as a mentor and source of inspiration. It delves into how Buffett's teachings, whether through his writings or personal interactions, have shaped the educational and career paths of aspiring investors and business leaders.

8.1.2 The Buffett Effect on Financial Literacy

Buffett has been a vocal advocate for financial literacy. This section examines the initiatives and educational programs supported by Buffett, aimed at improving financial understanding and decision-making. Case studies highlight specific efforts to promote financial literacy and empower individuals to make informed choices about their personal finances.

8.2 The Berkshire Hathaway Legacy

8.2.1 Employee Perspectives

Berkshire Hathaway's unique corporate culture has left a lasting impact on its employees. This section explores the perspectives of current and former employees, shedding light on the values, work environment, and experiences that define the Berkshire legacy. Interviews and anecdotes provide a firsthand account of the cultural impact of working within the conglomerate.

8.2.2 Shareholder Stories

The chapter delves into the stories of Berkshire Hathaway shareholders, examining the experiences and perspectives of those who have invested in the company over the years. Through interviews and testimonials, readers gain insights into the emotional connection shareholders feel toward Berkshire Hathaway and the ways in which their investments have shaped their financial journeys.

8.3 Cultural Contributions and Popular References

8.3.1 The Oracle of Omaha in Popular Culture

Warren Buffett has become a cultural icon, frequently referenced in literature, film, and popular media. This section explores the portrayal of Buffett in popular culture, from books and documentaries to fictional representations. It examines how the public perception of Buffett has evolved and the cultural impact of his status as the "Oracle of Omaha."

8.3.2 The Buffett Rule in Political Discourse

Buffett's advocacy for the "Buffett Rule" has had a significant impact on political discourse surrounding tax policy and income inequality. This section examines how the Buffett Rule has been discussed and debated in political circles, its reception among policymakers, and the broader implications for shaping economic policies.

8.4 The Philanthropic Legacy of Warren Buffett

8.4.1 The Giving Pledge in Action

Warren Buffett's philanthropic efforts have inspired a movement among the world's wealthiest individuals. This section explores the impact of the Giving Pledge, showcasing the philanthropic initiatives of signatories and the collective contribution toward addressing global challenges. It reflects on how Buffett's commitment to giving back has influenced a new era of responsible wealth stewardship.

8.4.2 Addressing Societal Challenges

Through the lens of Buffett's philanthropy, the chapter examines the ways in which his financial contributions have addressed societal challenges. Case studies explore specific projects and initiatives supported by Buffett, from healthcare and education to poverty alleviation and environmental conservation. It reflects on the broader implications of philanthropy in shaping a more equitable and sustainable world.

8.5 Reflections on Buffett's Legacy

8.5.1 Lessons for Future Generations

The chapter concludes with reflections on the enduring legacy of Warren Buffett. It distills key lessons from his life, career, and contributions to finance, philanthropy, and culture. Whether inspiring the next generation of investors, fostering a culture of transparency and integrity, or championing social responsibility, Buffett's legacy continues to shape the way individuals and organizations navigate the complexities of the world.

As we reach the final chapters of this exploration, subsequent sections will provide a comprehensive synthesis of Warren Buffett's impact on various facets of society, offering a reflective and forward-looking perspective on the lasting legacy of the Oracle of Omaha.

9

Synthesis and Future Perspectives

9.1 Synthesizing Buffett's Impact

9.1.1 Unifying Themes

This chapter begins by synthesizing the key themes that have emerged throughout the exploration of Warren Buffett's life, career, and legacy. It identifies the unifying principles that define Buffett's impact on finance, philanthropy, culture, and beyond. Through a comprehensive overview, readers gain a holistic understanding of the multifaceted legacy of the Oracle of Omaha.

9.1.2 Connecting the Dots

Building on the insights from previous chapters, this section connects the dots between Buffett's investment philosophy, leadership style, philanthropic endeavors, and cultural influence. It explores the interconnectedness of these elements and how they have collectively contributed to shaping Buffett's enduring legacy.

9.2 Future Perspectives: Navigating the Buffett Legacy

9.2.1 The Post-Buffett Era at Berkshire Hathaway

With Warren Buffett entering the later stages of his career, this section explores the challenges and opportunities facing Berkshire Hathaway in the post-Buffett era. It examines the company's approach to leadership succession, the potential impact on its investment strategy, and the ongoing relevance of Buffett's principles in guiding the conglomerate into the future.

9.2.2 Evolving Investment Strategies

The investment landscape continues to evolve, influenced by technological advancements, changing consumer behaviors, and global economic shifts. This section reflects on how the principles of value investing, economic moats, and long-term thinking—central to Buffett's approach—can be adapted to navigate the complexities of the modern investment landscape.

9.2.3 Philanthropy in the 21st Century

As philanthropy becomes an increasingly integral part of wealth stewardship, this section considers the future of philanthropy in the 21st century. It reflects on how the Giving Pledge, inspired by Warren Buffett's commitment to giving back, will continue to shape the philanthropic landscape and address emerging societal challenges.

9.3 The Buffett Legacy Beyond Finance

9.3.1 Educational and Inspirational Impact

Warren Buffett's legacy extends beyond financial success, influencing individuals worldwide. This section examines the educational and inspirational impact of Buffett's teachings, exploring how his principles continue to guide aspiring investors, business leaders, and those seeking financial literacy.

9.3.2 Cultural and Societal Contributions

The chapter delves into the broader cultural and societal contributions of Warren Buffett. It reflects on how Buffett's values, ethical business practices, and advocacy for responsible wealth distribution have influenced not only the business world but also the broader societal conversation about wealth, inequality, and social responsibility.

9.4 Lessons for Future Generations

9.4.1 Principles for Success

The chapter concludes with a reflection on the enduring lessons future generations can draw from Warren Buffett's life and legacy. Whether in the realms of finance, leadership, philanthropy, or cultural impact, Buffett's principles offer a timeless guide for individuals and organizations navigating the challenges and opportunities of an ever-changing world.

As we conclude this exploration of the multifaceted legacy of Warren Buffett, subsequent sections will provide a summary of key takeaways, reflections on the broader implications of his impact, and an invitation for readers to contemplate their own journeys inspired by the Oracle of Omaha.

10

Reflections and Invitations

10.1 Key Takeaways

10.1.1 The Legacy of Wisdom

This chapter begins by summarizing the key takeaways from the exploration of Warren Buffett's life and legacy. It distills the enduring principles that define Buffett's wisdom in finance, leadership, philanthropy, and cultural impact. Readers are invited to reflect on the lessons learned from the Oracle of Omaha.

10.1.2 Navigating Change

As we reflect on Buffett's journey, this section emphasizes the theme of navigating change. Whether in the context of the dynamic financial landscape, evolving leadership paradigms, or the societal challenges addressed through philanthropy, Buffett's ability to adapt and stay true to core principles serves as an inspirational model.

10.2 The Broader Implications

10.2.1 Beyond Finance

The chapter explores the broader implications of Buffett's impact, transcending the realm of finance. It reflects on how Buffett's emphasis on integrity, philanthropy, and responsible wealth stewardship has shaped cultural conversations, influenced societal norms, and inspired a new generation of leaders and investors.

10.2.2 Philanthropy as a Force for Change

Warren Buffett's commitment to philanthropy is examined in the broader context of societal impact. This section reflects on the role of philanthropy as a force for positive change, addressing systemic challenges and contributing to the creation of a more equitable and sustainable world.

10.3 Invitations for Personal Reflection

10.3.1 Your Own Investment Philosophy

Readers are invited to reflect on their personal investment philosophies. Drawing inspiration from Buffett's principles, this section encourages readers to consider their approaches to risk, patience, and the long-term perspective in the context of their own financial journeys.

10.3.2 The Power of Giving Back

The chapter extends an invitation to contemplate the power of giving back. Inspired by Buffett's philanthropic endeavors, readers are encouraged to explore ways in which they can contribute to positive societal change, whether through financial contributions, volunteerism, or other forms of impactful giving.

10.4 Your Journey Inspired by Buffett

10.4.1 Writing Your Story

As we conclude the exploration of Warren Buffett's legacy, readers are invited to consider how his life and principles have influenced their own journeys. This section encourages individuals to reflect on the chapters of their lives written in the spirit of Buffett's wisdom, leadership, and commitment to making a meaningful impact.

10.4.2 Continuing the Legacy

The chapter concludes with an invitation for readers to continue the legacy of Warren Buffett. Whether through responsible investing, ethical leadership, or philanthropic efforts, individuals are encouraged to carry forward the principles inspired by the Oracle of Omaha and contribute to a future guided by wisdom, integrity, and a commitment to positive change.

As this journey concludes, the reflections and invitations serve as a call to action for readers to apply the lessons of Warren Buffett in their own lives, shaping a future that embraces the enduring legacy of the Oracle of Omaha.

11

Beyond Buffett - Charting a New Course

11.1 The Evolution of Wisdom

11.1.1 A Continuum of Learning

This chapter begins by acknowledging that wisdom is an ever-evolving entity. It explores the notion that the principles and lessons drawn from Warren Buffett's life and legacy serve as a foundation for continuous learning and adaptation. Readers are encouraged to view wisdom not as a static destination but as a journey of perpetual growth.

11.1.2 Expanding Horizons

As we look beyond Buffett, this section reflects on the need to expand our horizons and embrace a diverse array of perspectives. It explores how the world of finance, business, and philanthropy is evolving, presenting new challenges and opportunities that demand a willingness to learn, adapt, and contribute to positive change.

11.2 The Shifting Landscape of Finance

11.2.1 Technological Acceleration

The chapter delves into the rapid technological advancements shaping the financial landscape. It explores the transformative impact of artificial intelligence, blockchain, and other emerging technologies on investment strategies, risk management, and the very nature of financial transactions.

11.2.2 Global Challenges and Opportunities

The financial world is increasingly influenced by global challenges, from climate change to geopolitical shifts. This section examines how these challenges present not only risks but also opportunities for responsible investing and strategic philanthropy.

11.3 Leadership in the 21st Century

11.3.1 New Paradigms of Leadership

As leadership paradigms evolve, the chapter explores the qualities and skills required for success in the 21st century. It reflects on how leaders can navigate complexity, foster innovation, and cultivate diverse and inclusive environments.

11.3.2 Ethical Imperatives

In an era of heightened awareness around ethical business practices, this section emphasizes the importance of leaders prioritizing integrity, transparency, and social responsibility. It explores how ethical imperatives are becoming central to organizational success.

11.4 The Future of Philanthropy

11.4.1 Social Impact Investing

The chapter explores the rise of social impact investing, where financial returns are pursued in tandem with positive societal outcomes. It reflects on how individuals and organizations can align their investments with a broader commitment to addressing social and environmental challenges.

11.4.2 Collaborative Philanthropy

In the evolving landscape of philanthropy, this section examines the power of collaborative efforts. It explores how partnerships, alliances, and collective initiatives can amplify the impact of philanthropic endeavors, addressing complex global issues more effectively.

11.5 Charting Your Own Path

11.5.1 Personal Agency in a Changing World

As readers look to the future, this section encourages a sense of personal agency. It explores how individuals can chart their own paths, drawing inspiration from Buffett's principles while adapting to the unique challenges and opportunities of their time.

11.5.2 The Enduring Legacy of Wisdom

The chapter concludes by emphasizing the enduring legacy of wisdom. It reflects on the timeless nature of principles such as patience, integrity, and the commitment to positive impact, inviting readers to carry forward the legacy of wisdom in their own journeys.

As we navigate the changing landscapes of finance, leadership, and philanthropy, this chapter serves as a guide for readers to not only learn from the past but also embrace the future with resilience, curiosity, and a commitment to making a meaningful difference.

12

The Legacy Unfolds - A Continuous Journey

12.1 Embracing a Continuous Journey

12.1.1 Wisdom in Motion

This chapter begins by embracing the idea that legacies are not static; they are dynamic, continuously evolving entities. It explores how the legacy of Warren Buffett unfolds through the actions, decisions, and contributions of individuals inspired by his wisdom. The concept of a continuous journey becomes a central theme.

12.1.2 Learning from Experience

As we reflect on the legacy of Buffett, this section emphasizes the value of learning from experience. It explores how individuals can draw insights not only from successes but also from challenges and failures, viewing each experience as a stepping stone on the journey toward wisdom.

12.2 The Power of Adaptation

12.2.1 Navigating Change

The chapter delves into the power of adaptation as a key element of unfolding legacies. It reflects on how individuals and organizations can navigate change, embrace innovation, and respond effectively to the evolving landscapes of finance, leadership, and philanthropy.

12.2.2 A Symphony of Perspectives

In the spirit of adaptation, this section explores the importance of incorporating diverse perspectives. It reflects on how the convergence of different viewpoints creates a symphony of ideas, fostering innovation and resilience in the face of uncertainty.

12.3 Amplifying Impact Through Collaboration

12.3.1 Collaborative Wisdom

As legacies unfold, the chapter explores the impact of collaborative efforts. It reflects on how individuals and organizations can amplify their influence by working together, forming partnerships, and collectively addressing complex challenges that transcend individual capacities.

12.3.2 Mentorship and Legacy Building

This section emphasizes the role of mentorship in legacy building. It explores how seasoned individuals can contribute to the unfolding legacies of others by providing guidance, sharing experiences, and cultivating the next generation of leaders and change-makers.

12.4 Sustaining the Spirit of Philanthropy

12.4.1 Philanthropy as a Continuum

The chapter examines philanthropy as a continuum within the unfolding legacy. It reflects on how individuals can sustain the spirit of giving by viewing philanthropy not as a one-time act but as an ongoing commitment to creating positive social and environmental impact.

12.4.2 Legacy Philanthropy

In the context of philanthropy, this section explores the concept of legacy philanthropy. It reflects on how individuals can design their philanthropic endeavors to endure beyond their lifetimes, leaving a lasting impact that contributes to the well-being of future generations.

12.5 The Endless Ripples of Impact

12.5.1 The Ripple Effect

As legacies unfold, this section explores the concept of the ripple effect. It reflects on how the actions and contributions of individuals inspired by Buffett's wisdom create ripples of impact that extend far beyond their immediate spheres, shaping the broader landscape of finance, leadership, and philanthropy.

12.5.2 The Ever-Growing Orchard

The chapter concludes by envisioning the legacy as an ever-growing orchard of wisdom. It reflects on how each individual's journey, inspired by Buffett's principles, contributes to the flourishing of this orchard, producing fruits of positive change that nourish the world for generations to come.

As we approach the conclusion of this exploration, this chapter serves as a reminder that legacies are not final chapters but ongoing narratives, shaped by the continuous actions and contributions of those who draw inspiration from the wisdom of the Oracle of Omaha.

13

Summary

In this comprehensive exploration spanning twelve chapters, we embarked on a journey to uncover the multifaceted legacy of Warren Buffett, the Oracle of Omaha. Here is a summary of the key themes and insights gleaned from each chapter:

1. Introduction: Unveiling the Oracle
   - Set the stage for the exploration of Warren Buffett's impact on finance and philanthropy.
   - Outlined the structure and focus of the subsequent chapters.

2. Beyond Berkshire Hathaway: Buffett's Financial Mastery
   - Explored the evolution of Buffett's investment philosophy and his unparalleled success with Berkshire Hathaway.
   - Examined key investment principles, such as value investing, economic moats, and the emphasis on long-term thinking.

3. The Berkshire Hathaway Legacy: A Conglomerate for the Ages
   - Delved into the history and structure of Berkshire Hathaway as a conglomerate.
   - Explored how Buffett's leadership and investment strategies contributed to the success and longevity of Berkshire.

4. Warren Buffett's Philanthropic Journey
   - Traced Buffett's philanthropic roots and the turning point leading to his significant pledge to the Gates Foundation.
   - Explored the Giving Pledge initiated by Buffett, encouraging wealthy individuals to commit to philanthropy.

5. Leadership and Legacy: The Buffett Effect
   - Examined Buffett's unique leadership style, emphasizing decentralized decision-making and integrity.
   - Explored the cultural impact of Berkshire Hathaway and addressed challenges and critiques of the Buffett model.

6. The Cultural Impact of Berkshire Hathaway
   - Explored Berkshire Hathaway as a cultural icon, analyzing its annual shareholder meetings and the sense of community among shareholders.
   - Examined Berkshire's corporate culture, values, and the shareholder-centric approach.

7. The Evolution of Finance: Navigating the New Normal
   - Explored the changing landscape of finance, driven by technological disruption and globalization.
   - Examined how Berkshire Hathaway is adapting to the digital age and the rise of sustainable finance.

8. Warren Buffett's Enduring Legacy
   - Explored Buffett's impact on individuals, emphasizing mentorship, education, and financial literacy.
   - Examined the cultural contributions and popular references associated with Buffett.

9. Synthesis and Future Perspectives
   - Synthesized key themes from Buffett's impact on finance, leadership, and philanthropy.

SUMMARY

- Explored future perspectives, including the post-Buffett era at Berkshire Hathaway and evolving investment strategies.

10. Reflections and Invitations
   - Encouraged readers to reflect on key takeaways and broader implications of Buffett's impact.
   - Extended invitations for personal reflection and continued legacy building inspired by Buffett.

11. Beyond Buffett - Charting a New Course
   - Explored the evolving landscapes of finance, leadership, and philanthropy beyond Buffett.
   - Emphasized adaptation, collaboration, and personal agency in navigating the changing world.

12. The Legacy Unfolds - A Continuous Journey
   - Embraced the concept of a continuous legacy, dynamic and evolving.
   - Explored the power of adaptation, collaboration, and sustained philanthropy in unfolding legacies.

Throughout these chapters, the exploration aimed to provide a comprehensive understanding of Warren Buffett's impact, not only on finance but also on leadership, culture, and philanthropy. The legacy of the Oracle of Omaha serves as an inspiration for individuals and organizations to navigate a changing world with wisdom, integrity, and a commitment to positive impact.

www.ingramcontent.com/pod-product-compliance
Lightning Source LLC
LaVergne TN
LVHW012130070526
838202LV00056B/5935